Lynton and its Coast

A Brief History

Lynton and its Coast

A Brief History

Ernest Mold

Illustrations by Edward Thornburgh

Tidicombe House, Arlington, Barnstaple, Devon

First published in Great Britain, 1992

With the exception of the binding materials, this book has been produced using re-cycled paper.

ISBN 0 9519622 0 5

Printed in Great Britain by
Arthur H. Stockwell Ltd.
Elms Court Ilfracombe
Devon

Contents

Map	6
The Rise from Obscurity	9
Lynton and Lynmouth	17
Countisbury	27
Parracombe	31
Martinhoe and Trentishoe	39
Blackmoor Gate	43
Envoi	45

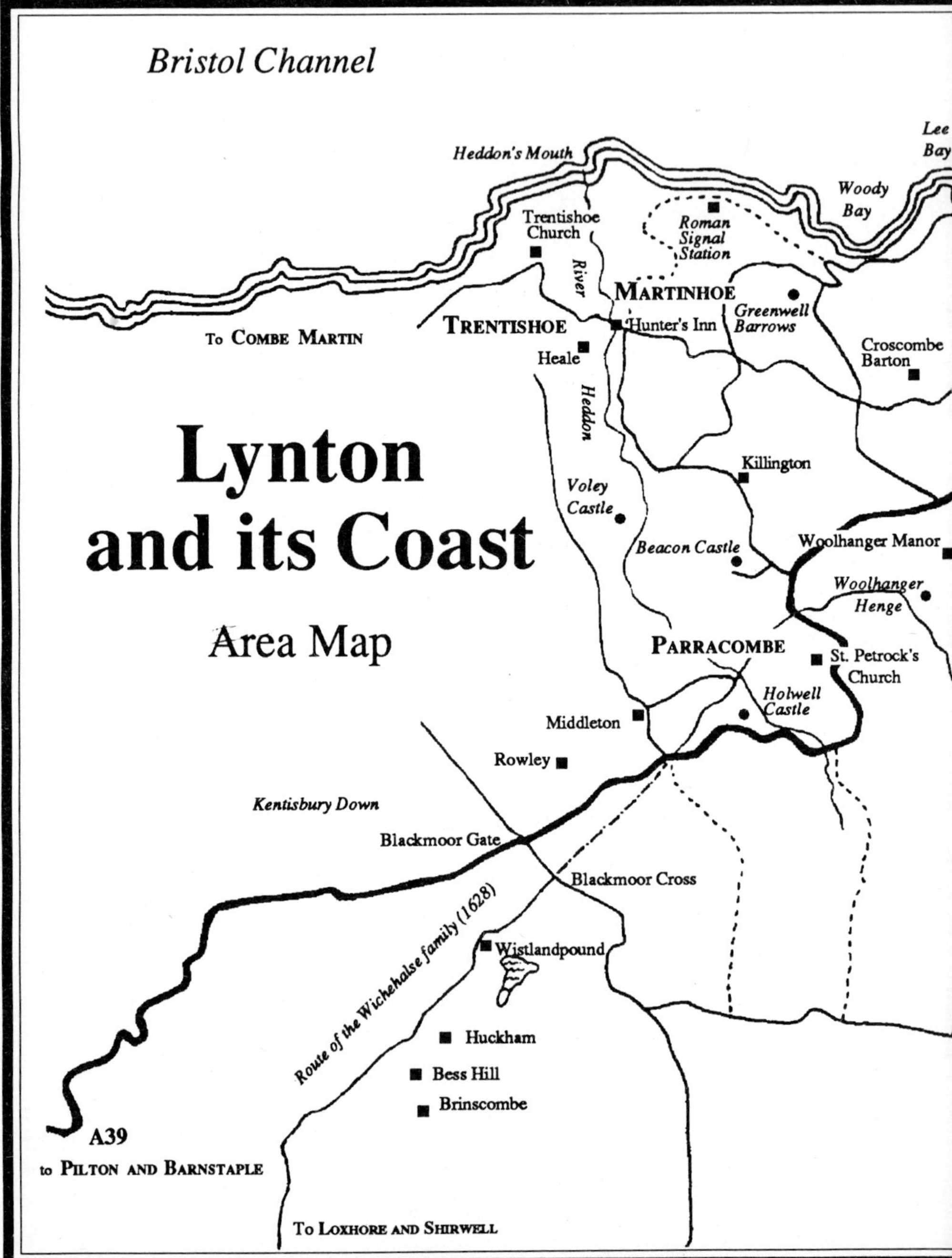
Bristol Channel
Lynton and its Coast
Area Map
Heddon's Mouth
Lee Bay
Woody Bay
Trentishoe Church
Roman Signal Station
River
MARTINHOE
Greenwell Barrows
TRENTISHOE
Hunter's Inn
To COMBE MARTIN
Heale
Croscombe Barton
Heddon
Killington
Voley Castle
Beacon Castle
Woolhanger Manor
Woolhanger Henge
PARRACOMBE
St. Petrock's Church
Holwell Castle
Middleton
Rowley
Kentisbury Down
Blackmoor Gate
Blackmoor Cross
Route of the Wichehalse family (1628)
Wistlandpound
Huckham
Bess Hill
Brinscombe
A39
to PILTON AND BARNSTAPLE
To LOXHORE AND SHIRWELL

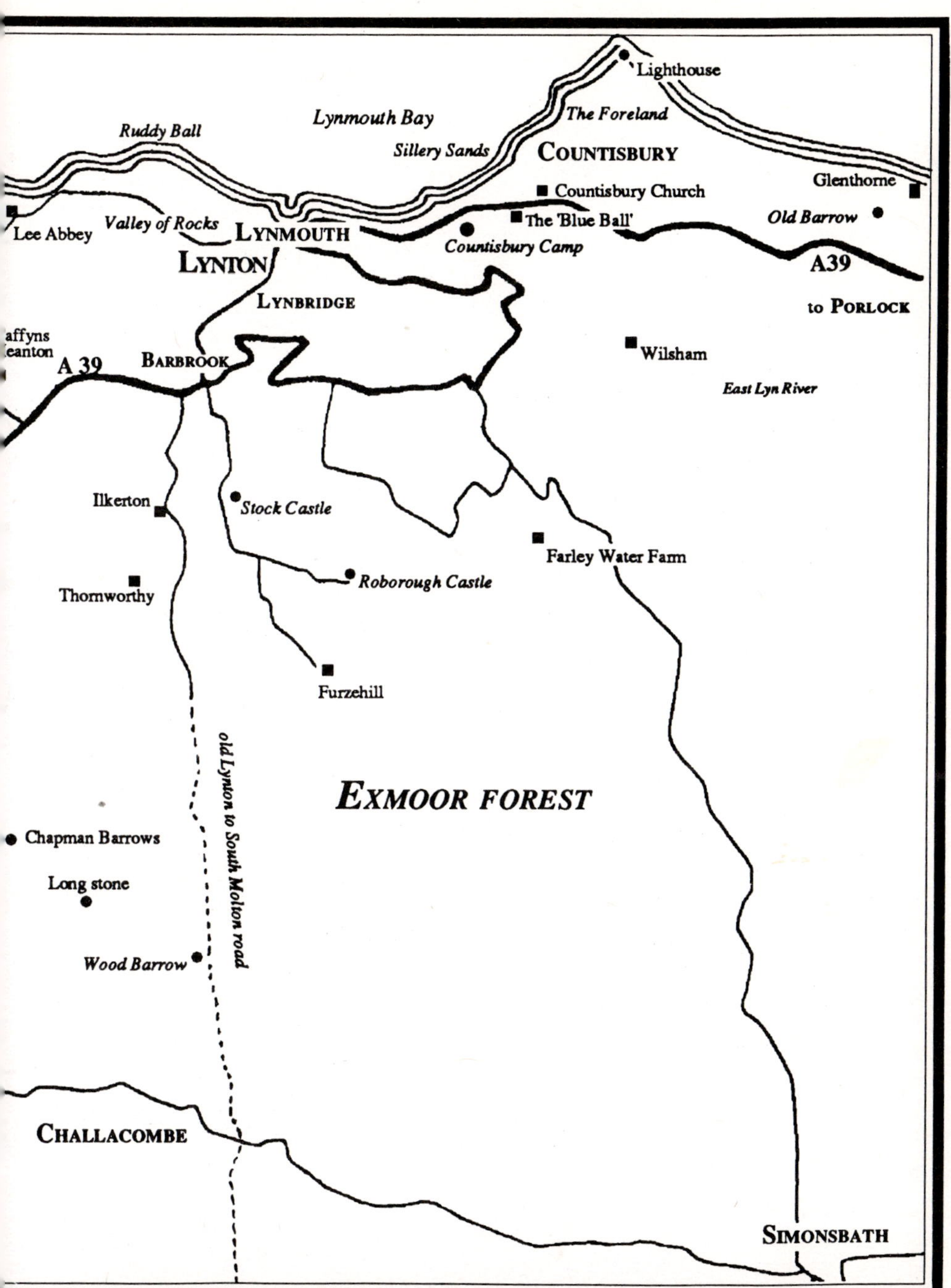
Lighthouse
The Foreland
Lynmouth Bay
Ruddy Ball
Sillery Sands
COUNTISBURY
Countisbury Church
Glenthorne
The 'Blue Ball'
Old Barrow
Lee Abbey
Valley of Rocks
LYNMOUTH
Countisbury Camp
A39
LYNTON
LYNBRIDGE
to PORLOCK
Wilsham
A 39
BARBROOK
East Lyn River
Ilkerton
Stock Castle
Farley Water Farm
Roborough Castle
Thornworthy
Furzehill
old Lynton to South Molton road
EXMOOR FOREST
Chapman Barrows
Long stone
Wood Barrow
CHALLACOMBE
SIMONSBATH

When the wind howls in the Valley of Rocks and the sea breaks over Quay Head or when both moor and sea are hidden in mist, imagination reaches back to the days when roads were merely bridle paths and boats depended on sail and oar alone to reach the safety of harbour. It seems that the coastal strip between, say, Combe Martin and Lynmouth was unknown and forbidding, isolated till the nineteenth century. The great and stirring events of English history, its joys and calamities, were probably but dimly realised here; even the Black Death, though it came close, seems to have passed it by. It had, however, a continuous quiet history of its own, slow to change - so slow that the evidence from each successive age is still visible.

The Stone Age people knapped flints on Kentisbury Down, leaving their chippings on the factory floor. They built a henge near Woolhanger Wood; other as yet undated and indeed unmapped earthworks nearby may yet be ascribed to them. The Bronze Age people made Exmoor their home for a thousand years and more. The weather, it seems, on the evidence of pollen analysis, was favourable in those days. They crowded their monuments - barrows, standing-stones, stone settings - along and just below the ridges, probably along the ancient ridgeways the Stone Age men first used, but they also extended them to the very cliff edge. The Longstone and Chapman Barrows dominate the hills above Parracombe but Greenwell Barrows at Martinhoe and the standing-stones at Lyn Down show that the coast was similarly populated. The Valley of Rocks at Lynton, fascinating today even with its traffic, shows rings of stones that can reasonably be assumed to be hut-circles. There was a reference in 1854 to the demolition of stone circles there to provide stones for gate-posts.

The Longstone

The Iron Age tribes lived in a less idyllic age. Perhaps they were a less idyllic people. Their contribution was of defended camps; Countisbury Camp, crowning the hill to the east of Lynmouth, is the best and biggest, with great ramparts on the side exposed to attack but a calm reliance on Nature - the steep drop into Chiselcombe and the Lyn Valley - on the other. It is perhaps best seen from the sea, when the full length of the defences down the cliff is apparent. Roborough Castle, just south of Lynton, is imposing even though parts of the earthworks were ploughed flat before the Man from the Ministry arrived and politely explained to the farmer what he was doing. Beacon Hill, on the Parracombe - Martinhoe boundary, is a good example of the simple Iron Age 'round'. Voley castle, just across the river Heddon and visible from the Beacon Hill camp, is not so easily identified; it may be Iron Age but its appearance is certainly not typical and it is in a poor if not impossible defensive position - to add to the confusion it has a big standing stone (of the Bronze Age?) nearby.

Stock Castle, over towards Furzehill, is thought to be later, perhaps second or third century A.D. (The term 'Iron Age' is poorly defined; the Celtic way of life hardly came to a precipitate halt - at any rate on Exmoor - merely because the Romans landed.)

The Romans did penetrate the area - just. They built a Signal Station at Martinhoe, still clearly traceable, to keep a watch on the warring tribes across the Bristol Channel. It was excavated in 1961 when its presumptive date - the middle of the first century A.D. - was confirmed. Evidence of wooden barrack huts was found; and of signal fires.

The next few hundred years were probably uneventful and doubtless unprogressive. The Dumnonii, the British tribe inhabiting Devon, seem to have been relatively peaceful. It appears that they resisted the use of coinage, preferring barter. In any case those of them living on the North Devon coast were unlikely to be much disturbed by the governing body at Exeter, the Roman Isca Dumnoniorum.

Perhaps the first sign of a new era was the coming of St. Petrock, the itinerant Celtic evangelist. It was the Celtic and not the Roman Church which first brought Christianity to England, or at all events to the West of England. St. Petrock was the son of a Welsh prince; his influence extended through Devon and Cornwall and finally to Brittany. He came to Parracombe - St. Petrock's Combe - in A.D. 550 or thereabouts and established a church there. The church was doubtless of wood, probably surrounded by an earthen bank. There is now, of course, no trace of it, but it is tempting to wonder if a low circular bank a short distance from the later Norman church has not some connection with it.

A hundred and fifty years later the Saxons came, spreading across from Taunton. They were farmers; they settled in isolated farmsteads and tiny hamlets in the combes. Most of the farms in the area have names derived from their language. Names such as Kibsworthy, Thornworthy, Holworthy (worthy meaning originally 'enclosure' - coming to mean farm-stead). Caffyns Heanton farm is named 'Hantone' in Domesday; when it was taken over by the Coffin - of Caffyn - family in the thirteenth century it was known as Coffins Heanton - Caffyns Heanton it is to this day. The Saxon incursion appears to have been slow-moving and, all things considered, peaceful. Maybe the Britons stayed and intermingled; maybe they retreated westwards.

Much about the same time the Viking raids began. The Danes seemed particulary inclined to harry the Bristol Channel shores; the coast suited their flat bottomed boats which could be beached readily in small coves far from organised resistance. The Anglo-Saxon Chronicle frequently mentions raids on Porlock and the Somerset ports. Defoe, speaking of North Devon, says 'Antiquity tells us long stories of the Danes landing on this coast.' It is possible that the odd adventurous boat ran ashore at, say, Heddons Mouth, raided briefly and savagely and retired rapidly. There is an apocryphal story of a quantity of bones found in the Heddon valley, though it does not seem possible to get any precise details.

One recorded battle did, however, take place with some certainty in these parts. In 878 A.D., when Alfred was at Athelney, Hubba the Dane landed somewhere on the North Devon or Somerset coast and engaged in battle with Odda, the Ealdorman of Devon, who defeated him decisively. Asser, King Alfred's historian, tutor and friend, gives a detailed account of this; his description supports the belief that the battle took place at Countisbury. Moreover, Asser says he visited the site some years later; it is pleasant to imagine him on top of Countisbury Hill, looking down on the tiny fishing village at the mouth of the Lyn.

When the Normans came, after the Conquest, they found a relatively settled and organised countryside. Alfred had striven to create a law-abiding community: he established a network of fortified positions - burghs - of which one was at Pilton near Barnstaple. The unit of administration was the Manor, which was much more than a farming estate - the Lord of the Manor must have been lord indeed. 'On the day that King Edward was alive and dead', as the picturesque rendering of the terse TRE of the Domesday Book shorthand goes, there were three principal manors making up Lynton parish - Line, Lintone and Crintone. (The Great Domesday was compiled at Winchester from information taken from each county: the Exeter Domesday - the Devon recordings - shows INCRINTONE, which was transcribed at Winchester as CRINTONE. INCRINTONE was the Norman scribe's interpretation of the Saxon name - which still survives as ILKERTON.) These manors were taken from their Saxon owners and given to William Chievre, as was the manor of Countisbury; he thereby became the effective ruler of the two parishes.

Two of the three manors of Parracombe (Rowley - the rough land - and Middleton - the middle settlement) went to the Bishop of Coutance, together with the manors of Martinhoe and Trentishoe. The third manor - Pedrecombe - went to William of Falaise, a kinsman of King William, doubtless a powerful man. There must have been a reason why he should have held this manor in isolation (he had other manors further afield); it could be speculated that he was given it in order to fortify a key point in the area. A bishop was supposed not to be a man of war; in any case the Bishop of Coutance seems to have had the pick of Devon manors: he would hardly be expected to take Parracombe seriously. After all he had a magnificent cathedral in his Normandy hill-top town to look after as well - it was still in the building - and he handed over at least some of his manors to a certain Drogo for supervision. But, whatever the reason, William of Falaise built a motte and bailey castle (now, and maybe then, called Holwell Castle by virtue of its holy well) down by the River Heddon, controlling the Heddon Valley and its access to the sea at Heddons Mouth.

The manorial system - the feudal system, in fact - developed over the next few centuries. One imagines that at first each separate manor, with its rigid divisions of serfs, villeins and bordars, (slaves, freemen farmers - but with obligations - and tied cottagers) was an independent unit, but that gradually the village - the Parish - became the unit, with collective responsibility, for instance, of sending so many men to the King's wars. The church was the centre of village life - underlined, perhaps, by the name 'Town Farm' for the farm by the church, as at Martinhoe and Trentishoe. The Normans built a fine church at Parracombe, still dedicated to St. Petrock. Lynton's church appears to have been built in the thirteenth or fourteenth century (at least there is no earlier evidence) and Lynmouth did not have one at all - it had to wait till the nineteenth century. It is difficult to know when Countisbury church was built; it is just possible that it has the longest continuous history of them all. Every village - probably every manor - had its mill. In a country of small but fast-flowing rivers and streams they were, of course, watermills. Names abound to perpetuate the memory of them - Barbrook Mill, Mill Farm, Bumsley Mill, Millhouse - and two, at Lynbridge and at Parracombe, were working within living memory. The one at Lynbridge (in use as a saw-mill at the time it was partly demolished in the 1952 flood) is presumably the same foundation as that mentioned as a 'new mill' in Domesday Book.

From early Norman times Exmoor was designated as a Royal Hunting Forest. The title implied 'Game Reserve' rather than Woodland. Countisbury, Lynton and the lands to the west were not included as the Forest boundary on the western side was taken as the county boundary, so that the Forest was wholly in Somerset - though it is doubtful whether anyone was absolutely sure at the time where, in its entirety, that boundary ran. But the existence of the Forest so close, to the south and east, had a great significance for the area. With its rugged coastline and further wild moorland to the west its isolation was complete and as time went on the ordinary life of the community became more and more involved with the domination of the Warden of the King's land. The Lords of the local manors had certain rather variable and limited privileges, such as being able to keep cattle in the Forest, but in return were obliged to attend meetings of the Swainmote - the Forest Court - upholding the laws and customs of the Royal estate. A fine was imposed for non-attendance. And the Forest boundary had to be perambulated periodically, and the 'meare stones' - boundary marks - maintained. Later on a convenient arrangement was made whereby the local farmers could graze their sheep in the Forest in the early summer months - for a fee. The fee was arranged annually and was announced to the towns and villages in a ceremony known as 'Crying the Moor'.

The villages - or, more precisely, the parishes - had their own commons where sheep and cattle could be grazed - in practice this meant the moorland stretching up to the forest boundary. Lynton Common ran from Hoar Oak to just beyond Saddle Gate, where it met Parracombe

Common to the west and Challacombe common to the south. These commons were unchanged until the Enclosure Acts of 1860 (Lynton) and 1862 (Parracombe). Rights and privileges on them were controlled by the Lords of the Manors but it seems that concessions were made from mediaeval times onward to individuals, allowing them to enclose small patches on which to grow rye. The custom probably explains many of the old banks and ditches on the moor.

And so the years rolled on, nothing changing very much. Lynton in, say, 1600 A.D. was still a place of no account. Apart from the church no building of that date or earlier survives. (This applies to the village itself, not to outlying places such as Woolhanger, Caffyns Heanton, East Lyn.) One imagines a collection of poor huts inhabited by poor people. Lynmouth was a small fishing hamlet, not truly distinct from Lynton, though maybe a little more prosperous.

Parracombe was more important and apparently extending. Bodley Cottage, built about that time, was described as 'situated between the town of Parracombe and the hamlet of Bodley'. East Bodley Farm, a fine solid farmhouse, bears a mid seventeenth century date. The Manor of Parracombe was held by the St. Albyns, a rich and powerful family. Earlier, Middleton had been held by the Courtenays, Earls of Devon; in 1646 the Lord was a Richard Ferris, of Barnstaple, who, in his will of that date, left 'an annuity of £10 to be paid to such able schoolmasters as should be appointed by the Mayor and Aldermen of Barnstaple to teach children of that town' as well as twenty pounds yearly 'towards the binding forth of such poor children of the said town of Barnstaple apprentices'. A road, still marked by a hedge line along a hollow way, ran from Blackmoor Cross (and by implication from Barnstaple) to continue as Parracombe village street. This road is referred to specifically in 1797 and less precisely in 1628 when the Wichehalse family journeyed from Barnstaple to Lynton to take up residence there. To their cost, they found it went no further; their baggage train had to cross wild and difficult moorland. Parracombe was becoming part of the expanding outside world while Lynton stayed in isolation.

The change came in the nineteenth century, due principally to the improvement in communication. The roads were still primitive enough (the Lynton to South Molton road, crossing the top of the moor at Woodbarrow, probably looked much the same then as it does now - a rough, stony track) but at least they existed. The Crown disposed of the

Forest, selling it to John Knight in 1818; provision was made for the construction of roads across it. Shelley came to Lynmouth at the beginning of the century, staying at a cottage then called'Woodbine'. William and Dorothy Wordsworth had, with Coleridge, visited Lynton in 1797; the fashionable gentry of London followed a little later, coming down in their carriages with a retinue of servants. They stayed in large houses round about (Combe Park, for example). Later the houses in Lynton's Lee Road (previously merely a track to the Manor House at Lee - afterwards called Lee Abbey - and Lee Bay) were built to accomodate the humbler people who followed them. Public coaches opened up the way to Ilfracombe and to Minehead, coping with the 'dreadful hills' by harnessing extra horses and, probably, by persuading the passengers to walk up the steep parts.

Countisbury Hill

The tourist industry was born. In 1862 Parracombe was still the dominant village in the area; the police station was built there in that year; Sergeant Bounce was appointed to maintain the law in the district - he sent one constable to Lynton. By 1900 the roles were reversed; Lynton had a Cottage Hospital, a fine new Town Hall, even an Electricity Works of its own, as well as a Railway Station, and was becoming known throughout the country.

Lynmouth became important too, but not so dramatically. Lynmouth had always had access to the sea; there had always been fish to catch, there was at least the possibility of coastal trade, and, to eke out the honest penny, there was always smuggling. The occasional wreck helped, though there is no evidence of deliberate wrecking. But now trade became brisk. Much of what Lynton required could be brought in more easily by sea than by land - coal, for instance, from South Wales - and a little fleet of trading ketches was built up. Farmers had realised the benefits of adding lime to their moorland soil and lime kilns were being built along the coast wherever a small boat could beach and at some places where it would seem that no boat could.

Lynmouth had its lime kilns. It also had a small 'barking' industry - using oak-bark to weather-proof rope and canvas - from scrub oak in the combes. Then there were oysters to dredge from the ledges off the Foreland (though no longer herrings, not at least in any quantity, for they had finally disappeared, some say in disapproval of the doings of the Parson who built the summer-house on Summer-house Hill. Earlier generations of fishermen, at times of shortage, had blamed excessive demands for tithes, on account of which the fish, abashed at causing so much trouble, had quietly swum away).

Till 1914, certainly, and perhaps decreasingly till 1939, Lynmouth was a proper little maritime port; it is only in recent years that tourists have been its main concern.

Lynton and Lynmouth

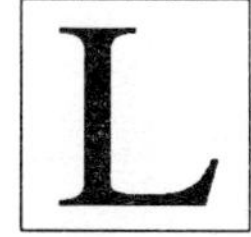

ynton and Lynmouth cannot, for the greater part of their recorded histories, be regarded as separate entities; they represented two aspects of the same parish, the hillside and the seaside, the farming and the fishing communities.

In the year 1200 or thereabouts the Saxon manor of Lintone, together with Countisbury manor and the little manor of Furzehill (mentioned for the first time) passed into the hands of Ford Abbey (the Church of St. Mary of Ford, a Cistercian foundation at Thorncombe, north of Lyme Regis on the Dorset border). The other manors remained in secular hands, became fragmented and passed through various ownerships. Line was split into two and eventually manor-houses were built at East Lyn and West Lyn. East Lyn, as Lower East Lyn Farm, though rebuilt here and there, survives still. Manor Farm, West Lyn, is at least on the original site. Willanger (now Woolhanger) appears in early mediaeval times as the largest holding in the divided Incrintona and is established as a full manor in Elizabeth's reign. The little manor of Caffyn's Heanton seems to have survived intact.

Thanks to its acquistion by Ford Abbey the manor of Lynton, as Lintone was now called, became the focal point of the parish and determined its future development. It was bounded by the West Lyn river, the coast and the little stream running down to Lee Bay. The Abbey held it for over three hundred years, till the Dissolution of the Monastries in 1536, and the successive abbots or their bailiffs must have given it stability and probably added to its wealth (though the common people were unlikely to have had much benefit from it). The herring fishery was flourishing and formed the basis of a coastal trade; the herrings were cured in huts known as Red Herring houses, on each side of the mouth of the river Lyn. The ancient law declared that the seaward limit of the manor was as far as a Knight on horseback, at mean low spring tide, could reach with his lance (perhaps a definition less precise than it seems given the vagaries of both tides and horses). Beyond that limit any subject of the King could take fish at will. But the Abbots claimed - successfully - to have the sole right of fishing to the 'middle thred of the River of Severne' - that is, half way to Wales. This by a convenient ecclesiastical argument presumably, that the Bristol Channel was not the sea at all but merely the estuary of the Severn.

At the Dissolution the Abbey was, of course, dispossessed. The bailiff at the time, however, was a layman and he continued to administer the manor for a different master - the King. Probably the change was hardly noticed by the inhabitants. Some twenty years later, in the second year of Queen Elizabeth's reign, the manor was sold to the Wichehalse family, merchants of Barnstaple. There was still to be no resident Lord of the Manor, however, and no manor house, until 1628 when Hugh Wichehalse, troubled over the possible recurrence of Plague in the town, left his Barnstaple house and made his perilous journey to Lynton. He made his home in an old farm-house near Lee Bay, extending and altering it to suit his needs. (It is now, many extensions and alterations later, known as Lee Abbey.)

Hugh Wichehalse, the first Lord of Lynton Manor actually to live there, seems to have been a pious and conscientious man, taking his turn as churchwarden and trying to do something to help the poor of the parish. And poor there must have been: a description of the village at the time tells only of the church on the hill and a few small cottages and a farm-holding - the Home-Tenement - below it. And, of course, an alehouse. The curate lived in what was little more than a hut.

It was believed to be the poverty, as well as the isolation, of Lynton which saved it from any involvement in the Civil War. Activity there was at Barnstaple and South Molton, but none nearer.

History did touch Lynton briefly, later in the century, when Monmouth's rebellion failed and the remnant of his defeated army scattered. Fleeing from Sedgemoor Nathaniel Wade, who commanded Monmouth's regiment in the battle, made his way to Ilfracombe and took a boat up-channel but was forced ashore near Lynmouth. Undetected, he managed to reach Hillsford Bridges (which might suggest that he landed on Sillery Sands) where he met a sympathiser, Grace Howe, who took him to Farley Water Farm: the farmer, John Birch, sheltered him but before long he was discovered and betrayed. The rector of Brendon gave information to the authorities: Brendon church was at that time situated at Cheriton, above Farley Water (it was removed, stone by stone, to its present site in the following century): the rectory, it is believed, was the present South Cheriton Farm, from which all goings-on at Farley could have been observed with a spy-glass. Anyway, Wade was captured, tried and, oddly enough, pardoned - but John Birch hanged himself. There is, incidently, a record of another of Monmouth's men being taken and killed in Bonhill Wood, just above Lee Bay. A broken 17th. century sword was found there a few years ago - it is now in Lynton Museum. Apart from such excitements the attention of the Wichehalses (Hugh died on Christmas Eve, 1653, as a touching monument in the church commemorates) was taken up by the affairs of the herring fishermen, who after all provided the chief source of their income.

To enter the harbour at Lynmouth can be difficult enough today if an awkward wind is blowing or a heavy ground sea running; in the days of dependence on sail or oar alone it must sometimes have been impossible. A quay of sorts had been built in Ford Abbey days and 'posts of great substance' had been set up to which vessels could make fast, but these were constantly being damaged or washed away. In 1607 a great flood had altered the course of the river and destroyed all the Red Herring houses and Curing pits on the Countisbury side. In 1769 a further flood was to jeopardise the foundations of the quay, smash up boats and fill the harbour with rocks. The battle with the sea was - is - unending.

Nevertheless, when the Wichehalses' financial position became strained and Countisbury Manor (which they had acquired with Lynton Manor - both had been managed as one estate since 1200 A.D.) was sold in 1679 to John Lovering, all fishing rights were retained: moreover that corner of Countisbury Manor between the river and the steep ascent of Countisbury Hill - the flat valley bottom and the foreshore - was also retained and added to Lynton Manor. In the 19th. century a later owner built his house there: the grounds are still known as "The Manor".

Things went from bad to worse for the Wichehalses. They were involved in law-suits: they were heavily in debt: finally in 1713 they lost all rights to the district, their property being acquired by Mr. John Short.

A bad time for the fishermen too. Mr. Short was unwilling to pour money into harbour repairs; the fishermen were forced to patch up the quay themselves as best they could. In retribution they refused to pay harbour dues. The herring shoals diminished. In 1750 the Red Herring Houses were shut down. Those on Merrill (or Mer Hill, perhaps truly Meare Hill, denoting the boundary, but anyway later confusingly called Mars Hill - doubtless a classical allusion, one would like to think with a touch of local humour) were turned into cottages. This may have provided modern Lynmouth with its most attractive feature but it marked the end of an industry which had thrived for centuries. The flood of 1769 was a culminating disaster; a despairing petition signed by local people implored the Lord of the Manor to repair the damage but it was not till years later that the harbour was satisfactorily restored. And nothing could persuade the herrings to return.

At the end of the eighteenth century the outlook for Lynmouth was bleak - for Lynton it had never been anything else. But the district had one great unassailable asset - its scenery. Inspired by the eulogies of the poets and perhaps discouraged from travelling in Europe so soon after the Napoleonic Wars the rich and notable came to visit. Lynton thrived and Lynmouth's sea-trade increased.

An engraving of 'Lynton Church and Village A.D. 1800' shows the little church on a wind-swept hill top, surrounded by rough stony ground, and a track winding down between a scatter of small squat cottages. An inn-sign hangs disconsolately from the corner of a darkly-etched wall; barrels litter its base. In the background are high imposing hills. A scene of desolation amid grandeur - doubtless as the artist intended. The track

leads down Pig Hill (Pig Hill Water, which gave the cottages their water supply, is not shown): nearly a century later, on the occasion of Queen Victoria's Jubilee, this track, now a proper recognisable road between houses, was renamed Queen Street in grateful recognition of the benefits her reign had brought.

As the villages became better known it became fashionable to paint, etch, make engravings and wood-cuts of them, and prints, of Lynmouth especially, abound. One dated 1814 shows Mars Hill much as it is now but no other street or road between it and the river; the only house shown there is Old Manor Cottage, then a single storey building, perched on a great rock overhanging the harbour. (The harbour was then, and indeed was till 1952, merely the mouth of the river, protected by the quay). Buildings and a lime-kiln are shown on the Countisbury side and a hint of more cottages further inland, beyond the confluence of the East and West Lyn rivers. The harbour seems trim and well cared-for; two sloop rigged vessels are shown at anchor and a red-waistcoated, hard top-hatted seaman sculling a cumbersome boat towards them. Two similarly dressed mariners on the quay sitting on a bollard and having a quiet nautical chat. No sign of stress. No sign of hurry. Perhaps artistic licence. Communication by road, however, was not so well advanced. In 1824 Mr. Sanford came to Lynmouth to take up residence at Clooneavin but his carriage could not complete the final part of the journey by ordinary means; it was hoisted on to the shoulders of local men who carried it bodily.

Later in the century Lynmouth Street was built, along the earlier - pre-1607 - course of the river. Built haphazardly perhaps, and piecemeal, but pleasantly enough; the houses on the east side rose literally from the river. Old Manor Cottage now had a road in front of it. Hotels were built to accommodate the visitors. General Rawden built the Rhenish tower on the quay-head, thus completing the familiar look of Lynmouth.

The village was probably at its busiest in the early part of the present century. Coal from Wales to be unloaded between tides, shovelled into carts waiting on the harbour bottom and hauled up the slipway. (It is said that it was when a vessel unloading coal was in juxtaposition with a vessel unloading flour - maybe as they were being cleaned out afterwards - that the traditional 'Miller and Sweep' contest, an essential feature of any Lynmouth gala or festival, was conceived. It takes the form of 'friendly' combat between occupants of dinghys loaded with bags of flour or soot respectively - the dinghys loaned by very well-motivated owners.) Limestone to be carried to the kilns, burnt and shovelled into farmers 'butts'. (It was very thirsty work, shovelling lime; the thoughtful farmer brought bottles of beer with him; it ensured full measure). When the tide came in there might be a ketch anchored off-shore, waiting to be warped in. The 'posts of great substance', which had been renewed so often, now had a specific purpose. It would notoften be possible - or safe - to attempt to enter the harbour under sail but the ketch could be hauled from post to post - from the Weir post which marked the Salmon Weir to the Half-tide post or the Perch post according to conditions, and on to the Eastern Pole from which a rope could be passed directly to the capstan on the quay. The owner would stand on the quay-head, directing operations, vigilant for his cargo.

Every now and then, on dramatic occasions when the surf was pounding the beach, the maroon would go off on the Manor, at night the paraffin flares would be lit, and the whole village would race to the sea-shore. The life-boat would be hauled from its shed, wheeled out on its carriage, and men and boys would seize the ropes and rush it down the specially-constructed slip, stumbling on the rocks and slipping on the seaweed, till it reached water deep enough to effect the launch. The crew, rightly heroes of the hour, would be sitting on the thwarts, long oars at the ready, the coxswain at the tiller-lines. In a north-west gale launching would be near impossible; the one occasion when it was out of the question and the lifeboat was hauled to Porlock has passed into enduring village history. At the height of the storm, with telegraph wires down so that no other help could be sought, horses were called for and willingly supplied and a great crowd helped to drag, push and urge on the boat. In the narrow places hedges and stone walls were knocked down; when the final descent of Porlock Hill was made, part of a cottage was demolished to allow a corner to be turned. The life-boat was launched in the comparative shelter of Porlock Weir and stood by the "Forest Hall" - which did, in the event, ride out the storm - for the rest of the night.

And, of course, there were visitors and their luggage to be fetched from the Minehead coach or from the railway station at Lynton. Meanwhile the machinery of the new Electricity Company, probably the earliest village electricity company in England, was clanking away by the high wall on the East Lyn river, throwing the lamp-lighter out of business, and the

Cliff Railway - such asimpleidea of linked cars with balancing water-tanks but nonetheless unique - was carrying on its platform that rather comic new invention the motor-car, which might snort its way into Lynmouth but would never get up the Hill without help.

Up Lynmouth Hill then, to Lynton, which was growing apace. Pig Hill cottages had, in Victoria's reign, been consolidated (or, more accurately, for the most part pulled down and rebuilt) into Queen Street and building had continued up the opposite hill and along Lydiate Lane, the old track that wound uphill to reach the little hamlet of Dean and then, in the old days, had ended abruptly in open moorland. Later still the track to Lee had been made into a residential road (for the visitors). The Cottage Hospital had been opened in 1874; before that, in 1869, a water supply for the village had been established, a water-tower (still standing) being built on Sinai Hill. Previously the village drew its water from Ladywell, a spring on the side of South Cliff, which ran - and still runs - down the hill. It was conducted underground into the village. Common access was from a basin (the spot is marked by a grating

outside Lloyds Bank, near the Valley of Rocks Hotel). In the second half of the 19th. century cholera was rife in the neighbourhood: in 1868 Dr. W. Clarke, concerned that it might spread to Lynton, established the Lynton Water Company to provide piped water to the village: he gave twenty shares of the newly-floated company "to the poor in perpetuity".

Another of Lynton's benefactors, in that age which combined altruism with a shrewd eye for business, was Sir George Newnes, the founder of "Titbits", who made his home in Lynton in the 1890's, building for himself the magnificent Hollerday House on the hill above the village and, later, the Town Hall as a gift to the community. Hollerday House was burnt down in 1913 (the calamity was maliciously but probably falsely ascribed to the suffragettes) but the grand drive to it survives, with its deep cutting, created with enormous labour to save his carriage horses the steep initial climb. He was also the instigator of the Cliff Railway, though he declined to underwrite the proposed - and planned - pier at Lynmouth. Associated with Sir George Newnes is the name of Bob Jones, a local builder, a remarkable man who constructed the Cliff Railway, the Foreland lighthouse (and later other lighthouses on the Welsh coast, across the water) the Town Hall and other buildings in Lynton, including the gracious Convent of Poor Clares at the western end of Lee Road.

The Poor Clares celebrated the first mass in their new home on St. Joseph's Day, the nineteenth of March 1910. They had come from Rennes, in Brittany, a few years before to escape persecution, first settling in Woodchester and subsequently moving to Prospect House, at the bottom of Lynmouth Hill, to await the completion of their promised convent. They were, of course, French-speaking: the rules of their order were strict, by later standards perhaps even harsh: the sisters have, however, since then, played a quiet and retiring yet influential and greatly respected part in the life of the village.

The narrow-gauge railway to Barnstaple was opened in 1898 (though beaten to the post by the Cliff Railway in 1890) and Sinai Hill acquired new importance as porters plied their luggage-barrows to and from the station. (But the coaches still ran, as they were to do for many years yet; as late as 1919 the Minehead coach would pull out of Porter's Yard each morning and bowl along Lee Road, Mr. Carey, the guard, resplendent in his red coat, playing 'Anchors Aweigh' on the coach horn.)

Lynton was still a village, though, with a village life, and could turn out in force to celebrate the Relief of Mafeking, with banners flying, and could hold Friendly Society marches in the streets, and Pony Shows and competitions in the fields between Lee Road and Lydiate Lane. It ran a Parish magazine, in which a very Victorian moral serial story competed with more vivid accounts of life-boat rescues, flower-shows, regattas, the opening of the Esplanade by the Lady of the Manor and scholastic achievements at the village school. It had, however, come a long way since 1800.

It is not so different today really. A few more streets, a few more houses, a great many more cars. Railway closed in 1935, but the Cliff Railway as popular as ever.

Lynmouth might have kept its quaint, tumbling character, too, if it had not been for the devastating flood of 1952, which swept houses and lives away. Radical re-planning, shifting of the river's course, and a new concept for the harbour and provision of car-parks changed it dramatically. But perhaps it could not have survived the Motor Age as it was, anyway.

August 15th, 1952

It had been a wet summer: the moor - a thin layer of peat barely covering impermeable rock - was sodden. Its little streams were swollen and overflowing. In August the rain fell heavily, relentlessly, continuously. The swollen streams suddenly became torrents, rolling down great boulders and tearing down trees. The countless tributaries of the River Lyn combined to produce an unimaginable wall of water which engulfed Lynmouth. Bridges were first blocked, damming the flood, then swept away. Every riverside house was damaged; some were demolished entirely. Twenty-eight lives were lost. It was a night of chaos, confusion and unsung individual heroism.

Countisbury

Countisbury plays apples to the historian's Tantalus; so many answers are snatched from his grasp. That there was an ancient Bronze Age - perhaps Stone Age - track along the ridgeway, approximating to the modern main road, seems certain; barrows and standing stones testify to it. A Beaker period - about 2000 B.C. - skeleton was found interred in a stone kist at the head of Deddycombe. (It is now in Taunton Museum). But where did the track go to? Billing's Directory of 1857 says; 'We find Countisbury marked on the most ancient maps of England, with a road over Exmoor to Molland' - but affords no further evidence.

The massive rampart of Countisbury Camp is undoubtably of Iron Age construction (perhaps three hundred years or so B.C.); it was probably still maintained long after the Romans came to Britain. It is believed to be the site of the battle of Arx Cynuit in 878 - the description fits well enough. The early mediaeval records of Ford Abbey do, apparently, refer to "the heathen burial ground at Countisbury". It would be heartening to find Hubba's burial mound or a few lost battle-axes. It it were so, how did the Danes approach? Up from Sillery Sands or more cautiously from Porlock?

Porlock was of much more importance as a landing place than now, in the early days: the Anglo-Saxon Chronicle details at least one Viking raid there. And not only the Vikings: it records that in 1052 Earl Harold - later, briefly King - quarrelling with the then King, Edward the Confessor, raided Porlock and harried inland. Doubtless to plunder the rich Porlock Vale but the people of Countisbury must have watched from the cliffs with apprehension.

Old Barrow, above Glenthorne, was a Roman signal station, manned for a short time only and, apparently, abandoned in favour of Martinhoe. Perhaps the mists were too frequent. So much is established beyond serious doubt but details would be fascinating; did the centurion march his men up Porlock Hill? Did he beach flat-bottomed boats at Glenthorne?

Then the church. It was referred to in the thirteenth century but it has been entirely rebuilt, piecemeal, in the course of the last two hundred years. There is a strong belief that it is a Saxon foundation but evidence is lacking.

The parish records are of little help. They, too, only go back two hundred years and are much more concerned with the price of beer (Nails 3d. ; Ale for the Mason 2s.6d.) than with less pressing matters. There are, however, two pleasing furnishings left in the chancel rebuilt by Walter Halliday in 1846: an elegant classical screen dated to about 1700 and a fifteenth century carving in oak showing a chained swan above the arms of the Courtenays, Earls of Devon. It was disappointing, though, to discover a letter, written more than a hundred years before by Halliday's widow, stating that the screen was purchased at an auction (it had originally been installed in Chittlehampton church). It is a fair assumption that the carving - a bench end - was acquired by the same, or similar, means.

The inn claims to date from mediaeval times. The building - originally three cottages - may well do so but it seems to have become a hostelry in about 1800. Though a traveller who had made his way across the top from Porlock or who had just climbed Countisbury Hill might look for a little refreshment in any age. Maybe it was a Church House. Very recently, without obvious reason, its name changed but it was known to many generations of local people as the 'Blue Ball'. Did this name refer to the round-topped heather-covered hill the inn snuggles under or to an obsolete navigation aid which, apparently, when hoisted amounted to an invitation to enter harbour? Or, more simply, did the sign represent the traditional fishing-net float painted blue to deceive the fishes?

The reliable recorded history of the parish dates from the entry in the Domesday Book. It is inseparable from the history of Lynton till the Wichehalse family finally parted with both manors in 1713. Thereafter Countisbury had no true Lord of the Manor until over a hundred years later. D. and S. Lysons in 1822 (Magna Britannia) pronounce; 'There is no manor in the parish'.

The farm-houses had grown up along the ridge: Coombe, Ashton and Dogsworthy are all mentioned in the fourteenth century. Wilsham, down in the combe, was presumably a Saxon hamlet. The mill was at the edge of the parish, actually at Brendon but on the Countisbury side of the East Lyn (the boundary): despite the streams tumbling into the sea, water has always been in poor supply on the uplands.

Countisbury became something of a unit, perhaps for the first time, when, towards the middle of the nineteenth century, the Rev. Walter Halliday acquired Coscombe - renaming it Glenthorne - and subsequently most of the land in the parish. He benefited from the Enclosure Acts, improved the farming, extended the church and constructed a lime-kiln on the cliff-face below Rodney. He built a quite delightful house by the sea (though his coachman might have had reservations about the drive). He was a proper squire.

All this was not achieved easily. Over the years rights and titles had become confused, boundaries blurred. The ancient system of granting patches on the common to old retainers for growing a few crops of rye had, in the absence of proper manorial control, been abused. It was difficult to identify the owner of any particular property - though not for the lack of claimants.

Social conscience had been stirring a little before this, however. Round about 1819 the Poor House, a cottage still standing adjacent to the church, was seen be inadequate and an imaginative purpose-built replacement was established at Ducombe, down the hill towards Wilsham. A huge central chimney with four wings of two stories, rather like a Norman cruciform church, enabled one great blazing fire to heat the eight rooms.

The last, or latest, phase in Countisbury's colourful history includes the overland launch of the Lynmouth life-boat in 1899. A stop at the 'Blue Ball' was, of course, obligatory. (The Minehead coach stopped there to change horses every day.) Less glorious, but calling for even more prolonged effort, was the building of the lighthouse round about the same time; the labourers walked from Lynton in time to start the day's work at seven-thirty in the morning; for very little pay.

Parracombe

In 1876 Arthur Smyth, a Parracombe man, wrote a detailed account of his village, describing it farm by farm, house by house and adding a few revealing anecdotes of past and present inhabitants. A similar review written in, say, 1950 would have shown remarkably few changes. Most of the new houses and bungalows have appeared in the last thirty years.

At the time Parracombe Common had been recently enclosed: it had previously been part of the Manor of Parracombe Mill - the old manor of Pedrecombe. The Lord of the Manor then relinquished his title in exchange for a parcel of land: it was the end of an era. Four acres of the common were left unenclosed 'for exercise and recreation of the inhabitants of this parish.' It seems an unlikely gesture in a land-hungry age but Parliament had recently been throwing out Bills of Enclosure from too-greedy applicants; maybe the four acres served as a carefully calculated palliative. Despite an Inquiry in 1910: 'This is not used for any purpose and is quite unproductive' the 'Pleasure Ground' is still an unfenced tangle of bramble, gorse and Rose-bay Willow Herb.

Down in the village, meanwhile, the two inns were flourishing. The 'Fox and Goose' was then a low thatched building; it was to be rebuilt in 1894; it was already beginning to overshadow its rival, partly, at least, owing to the advent of wheeled traffic. Carriages were appearing as roads improved and carts were being used instead of the sledges which previously had been the standard conveyance on the moor. There was more room - and flatter ground - outside the 'Fox and Goose'. The Barnstaple - Lynton coach stopped there. But the other inn, too, had received a fillip. The Prince of Wales had called there for refreshment when he was following hounds locally. (He enjoyed hunting on Exmoor: a bog 'out over' from Oare still bears his name; regally ignoring advice, he tumbled into it). So the London Inn, as it had been called for years, became the 'Royal Hotel'.

The London Inn - Royal Hotel - stood (the house still stands) on one side of the small triangular patch of cobble-stones doggedly referred to as 'The Square'. Hard by was the Malt House, doing good business, and the recently built brewery, destined to produce mineral water as well as

Parracombe Ale until well into the next century. (When the foundations were being dug fine specimens of silver-lead ore were found; later a trial shaft was sunk in an adjoining field and a mining prospectus issued but the project came to nothing.) Across the street was the mill, its wheel turning steadily as the farmers rode in with sacks of corn across their ponies' backs. The mill-pond, fed by a leat from the River Heddon, was a little higher up the road, where the lane to the church turned off.

The new church had not yet been built but a year or two later the old church, St. Petrock's, was declared unsafe. Proposals to demolish it were denounced country-wide, particulary by John Ruskin, who donated ten pounds towards a new church in order to preserve the old. So preserved it was though used less and less frequently. It is a fascinating church. St Petrock, in the middle of the sixth century, built a structure of wood or

St. Petrock's

wattle and daub. It is likely that the Saxons erected a more permanent one, perhaps, again, of wood. The Norman William of Falaise, on acquiring the Manor, built what is now the nave of the present church. The tower was added in 1182 and the chancel in 1252. Some alterations were made in the fifteenth century, when the south aisle was added. (The fifteenth century was the great period of church rebuilding, owing to the increase in wealth from the wool trade; fortunately the Gothic had reached its peak in the Perpendicular style). Various renovations have been made since, notably when lightning struck in 1908, but they have been made with care. Inside, the church is still more interesting; the fittings have been kept much as they were in George the Third's time - screen, painted tympanum, box pews, musicians gallery andthree decker pulpit. The font,probably Norman, has a curious history. It was found, half-buried, in the rectory garden at Martinhoe in 1905 and was installed here.

The cottage by the church, altered again and again through the years, is the sixteenth - possibly fifteenth - century Church House. Church Houses were built during these two centuries as parochial meeting-places; they combined the functions of the parish hall and the 'pub' replacing the old manorial 'Lord's Brewhouse'. Parish Feasts were held there. Maybe they were rowdy places at times. Thomas Nashe, the Elizabethan dramatist and contentious writer, cried out, in his 'Christ's Tears over Jerusalem': 'Hath not the Divell hys Chapel close adjoining to God's Church?'

The rectory, in Arthur Smyth's day, stood below the church, in the shelter of the hill, surrounded by the glebe. (It is now, as Heddon Hall, in secular hands.) The extensive glebe (land appointed to the church) was culled from the Manor; its bounds were the lane from the church to the Lynton Road - Sentery, or Sentry, lane - the Lynton road itself, down to the mill-pond, and the lane - Church Lane - back to the church. The customary Sunday-afternoon walk, along the boundary, is still called 'Sentry Walk'. 'Sentry' perhaps in its obsolete form as a variant of 'Sanctuary": in the Middle Ages a fugitive from justice would be safe - for a time - if he could reach the church, or even grasp the iron ring - the Sanctuary Knocker - on the church door.

When the Rev. John Pyke was rector (1826 - 1868) the rectory must have been a very fine place indeed, with ornamental gardens, fish ponds and an 'Orchard House' for fruit. He converted the existing rectory into stables and built a new one - the present house.

The carriage drive for the Rectory met Church Lane at its junction with Bodley Lane by the school. There a few cottages formed the little settlement known as Prisonford - now, euphemistically, Prestonford. There is a trickle of a stream to provide the ford but the prison can only be guessed at. Thomas Westcote - 'A View of Devonshire', in 1630 - says of Parracombe Manor; 'To the Lord whereof belonged great power and privilege, and had a prison and execution of offenders within itself'. Maybe here.

Up the road, at Sunnyside Farm, there was formerly a Tucking Mill. The farm track is shown as 'Tucking Mill Lane' on old maps. Tucking was the finishing process by which the woven cloth was both cleansed and felted. Some sort of power was needed: here, it is said, it was provided by a heavy roller turned by a capstan bar to which a horse was harnessed, rather in the fashion of the cider presses commonly used in Normandy.

The lane affords a splendid view of Holwell Castle, down below, a 'motte and bailey', the earliest form of Norman castle construction. The motte - the mound which would have boasted a wooden keep, the last bastion of defence - stands proud; the Inner Bailey - the apron-like enclosure in front of and around it, forming a large courtyard - has its banks intact and the Outer Bailey - the overall defence area down to the river - is at least traceable. From the castle a handful of men-at-arms and archers would have dominated the valley and, particularly, the way up from the sea at Heddon's Mouth.

Holwell Castle

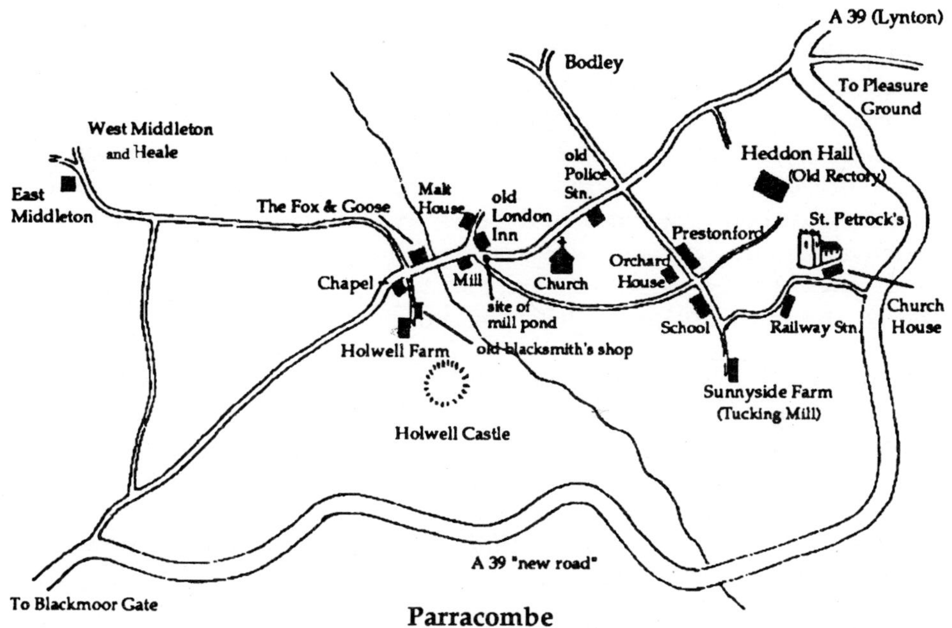

Parracombe

Not far away, by contrast, stands the Wesleyan chapel, built in 1839, in the heady days of Wesleyanism. It is a comfortable, solid structure, its architecture early enough to be simple and unpretentious. The Wesleyan movement had a great influence on village life, perhaps particularly so in the West Country, but it may have hindered progressive reform by its doctrine of acceptance of what it saw as God's Will. It certainly created schisms, not only between the chapel and the public house, but between Chapel and Church. The effect lingered on, in Parracombe as elsewhere.

To the north of the village lies a more secluded part of the parish, known to few except those who farm it or hunt over it, the lands of the old manor of Middleton. It is essentially a high ridge terminating in the strangely named Vention - formerly Invention - Hill, whose wooded slopes run down to the Heddon and Trentishoe Water valleys. It harbours isolated farms: Voley, warm and sheltered, which may have been the 'bird place' and so may have housed the fowler who snared or shot them; Walner, neighbouring, in the woods: the little settlement tucked away at Heale: Bumsley Mill down by the river. Voley Castle, the enigmatic circular enclosure whose age is undetermined, lies, with its standing-stone, on the slope down to the Heddon.

Arthur Smyth mentions the Annual Fair for cattle, sheep and horses, first held in 1856, still well-attended in his day, and the Whitsun Revels, which apparently had lapsed. (They have now been revived, though not quite in the old style: Mr. Smyth notes drunkenness and wrestling matches as prominent features in the old days.) He does not mention another discontinued tradition though the Rev. J.F. Chanter, some time later, records being told of it: in the early years of the century a football match took place annually between Parracombe and Martinhoe, the pitch three miles of open moorland from Parracombe churchyard to Martinhoe church, the rules, one imagines, elementary.

Wrestling, as R.D. Blackmore indicates in 'Lorna Doone', was a West Country pastime, perhaps at its height in the first half of the last century. A native of Parracombe, over ninety years old when he died several years ago, used to talk of his grandfather, who would tell him of fearsome trips to Cornwall 'wrastling' and invite him to feel his shins, scarred and notched with frequent kickings. All the village lads would ride down together - 'tweren't safe, else'.

A more recent picture of village life can still be had, first-hand, from men who were boys after the First World War. The roads were unmetalled and gated. Cars are not mentioned but excursions by horse-drawn brake - the precursor of the motor char-a-banc - were frequent. Pennies could be earned by fastening skids on the wheels at the top of the hill - and taking them off at the bottom - fetching water for the horses from the river in big wooden pails, opening gates......

The Barnstaple - Lynton railway was running on its narrow-gauge track. It puffed its way through the cutting, whose banks, early in the year, spelt 'Parracombe' in snowdrops, as it slowed down for the little station by the church.

The carpenter had a saw-pit up the Heale road; a long trench six foot deep straddled by beams. A tree-trunk, trimmed of branches, would be rolled on to them and marked out for cutting into planks. The top sawyer would take his massive coarse-toothed saw by its cross-handle and stand on the end beam while the bottom sawyer would scramble down into the flying saw-dust.

The Wheelright worked up Holwell farm lane, beside the stream which was fed by the Holy well. The wheel's rim was formed of separate arcs of wood known as felloes or fellies - 'vallies' in the dialect; the spokes were slotted into them and into the hub. (Terms long-used, as in Hamlet: "Break all the Spokes and Fallies from her wheel'.) The iron tyre held them together; it was heated red-hot, carried with tongs by a man and a boy and dropped precisely over the circumference. Then cooled rapidly with water from the stream. The concrete platform on which all this took place was, till recently, still standing there.

At prescribed intervals the parish bounds would be beaten. The boys would be initiated, having the marks pointed out to them so that the knowledge would not be lost. There is still a stone (though no longer upright) on Beacon Hill, by the Iron Age rampart, with 'P' on one side and 'M' (for Martinhoe) on the other; from there the boundary ran down to 'a big thorn tree' and then straight down to the river, where was a large hollowed stone into which water from a spring flowed. The boundary-beaters solemnly drank from it. In 1952 the flood washed it away, with much else.

Martinhoe and Trentishoe

Martinhoe, regarded as merely the cluster of buildings round the church, is no more than a hamlet. Martinhoe parish, however, includes a wide and interesting tract of country with access to the sea at Heddon's Mouth and Woody Bay. Topographically it is rather like Lynton; historically it was probably rather more favoured; it simply missed the tourist boom and so retained, more or less, its mediaeval pattern.

Greenwell Barrows, now flattened almost to obscurity, little known and rarely visited, must once have dominated the moorland that became Martinhoe Common. They form a scattered group rather than a row and are numerous enough to argue a well-established Bronze Age community.

The Iron Age Celts, who left their mark at Beacon Camp, on the hill above Parracombe, displaced the men who built the barrows and were then in turn displaced by the Saxons. In a brief interlude, round about A.D. 50, the Romans had visited Martinhoe and built their signal station, keeping stern watch over the sea.

By the time the Normans came the principal features of the neighbourhood were probably already in being. There were two Saxon manors, Chenoltona, now Killington, and Matingeho itself. Both appears in Domesday. Craddokescombe, or 'Cradoc's Combe' - now Crosscombe Barton - should indicate an even earlier Celtic settlement. Cradoc, or Caradoc, is more familiar in its classical form of Caractacus - though others than the British prince may have borne the name. Kemmacot, as Chymecote, is mentioned in 1330. Kittitoe - Ketecote - in 1244. Ranscombe - Rammescumbe - in 1249 and Mannacot - Manecot - in 1219. Slattenslade - Slatynslade - escapes notice until 1544 but probably did, in fact, exist much earlier. This is the pattern of early mediaeval settlement - isolated farmsteads and small hamlets in the combes, virtually self-sufficient. Kemmacot, today, exemplifies this - especially when the snow falls.

Thomas atte Mill, remarked upon in 1333, possibly plied his trade at Milltown; the stream still running beside Milltown Cottage would have suited a primitive mill. Mill Farm, a little higher up the valley, with a more elaborate leat, may be of later date though the present farmhouse has a stone staircase that would do credit to a Norman Keep. It was still grinding corn at the end of the last century. Between Mill Town and Mill Farm is a cottage that was once a Tucking Mill, where the woven cloth was 'finished' by a process of stretching and beating. Maybe the ground between the cottage and the bend in the river Heddon, now a garden, was the site of these activities.

The Church, Early English in style, seems to date from about 1300: It was heavily restored in 1866, when the musicians' gallery and other features were removed and the north aisle built. It has a memorial to Hugh Wichehalse's daughter Margaret, who died in 1683, and others to later members of the Blackmore family (Margaret had married Richard Blackmore: a branch of the family was to produce the novelist a century and a half later). Maybe there was an earlier church; the list of rectors goes back to the thirteenth century. And would the Bishop of Coutance, who held both manors, suffer an estate without a church? Apart from the evidence of the Norman font, so unceremoniously tossed into the Rectory garden, to be found there in 1908. (The rectory is now in secular hands; in its grounds is a building which may have been a mediaeval church house.)

Across the road stands the cottage which was opened as the National School in 1873, at the instigation of the Lord of the Manor. At some point, presumably previous to this, the church vestry, built in 1851, was used as the schoolroom. Opposite, the Parish Hall commemorates Bishop Hannington, who achieved fame as a missionary martyr when he was killed in Africa a hundred years ago. At one time he was curate to Martinhoe; he was fascinated by the cliffs near the church and constructed a path down to 'Hannington's Cave' below. At first he employed (or cajoled) labourers from the village but when the enterprise proved too hazardous for them he finished it himself.

Some concessions were made to the tourists. Hunters Inn was the earliest. It was originally a thatched cottage, probably little more than an ale-house; it was customary for parties to come over the cliffs from Combe Martin, hunting - or in this case shooting - foxes before regaling themselves with a barrel of beer at the inn. In 1895 the inn caught fire and burned down and was subsequently rebuilt in a more ornate style. The tale is told that, although the blaze was devastating, at least the barrel of beer was rescued and brought out, aflame but unbroached.

The discreet Glen Hotel was opened in 1893; it flourished and became better known as the Woody Bay Hotel, though the Inkerman Way Refreshment Rooms have disappeared. As has Woody Bay pier, planned to allow gentlemen in boaters and ladies with their parasols to step dryshod from the paddle steamers, to be met, doubtless, by suitable conveyances. It survived a bare five years; the supporting wall is still to be seen.

Trentishoe, across the Heddon valley to the west, has higher and steeper hills, is smaller and more remote but historically has much in common with Martinhoe. Up to a point. A few Bronze Age barrows on Trentishoe Down, two Domesday manors - Trentishoe itself (again, a prerogative of the Bishop of Coutance) and Tattiscombe, now a rather isolated farmhouse - and a tiny church not far from the cliff-edge. But whereas Martinhoe has survived change - indeed thriven upon it - Trentishoe has become a dwindling community. The casual motorist sees nothing but the splendid road over the hills by the sea: the few cottages and farms are hidden in the woods or in the combes and there is nothing more than a lane leading to the church. The mill down by Trentishoe Water is remembered only by its name. The lime-kiln at Heddons Mouth (the river is the parish boundary) serves only as a casual shelter and there is no inn, of even the memory of one. But the scenery is unsurpassed and the little winding roads completely unspoilt.

It might all have been different had an impossible dream come true; a speculator at the end of the last century evolved a scheme to build rows of villas on Holdstone Down, just over the parish boundary. One or two were built and still struggle with the elements; the rest are embryonic numbers scratched on stones, half-hidden by bracken and gorse.

Trentishoe may not have been well placed to benefit by tourism but it was a perfect place for smuggling. Heddons Mouth was convenient and easy, and doubtless used, but perhaps a little obvious. The cliffs to the west are, with some reason, held to be unscalable, but this is not absolutely true. Maybe self-interested folk-memory perpetuates the belief. A local man could manage Bosley Gut, even with a keg of brandy on his back. The churchyard was the traditional immediate hiding place; the little white flowers of Cardamine Trifolia grow, or used to grow, there; they are not indigenous: could the seed have come from France, brought over on muddy contraband?

The church, standing on a little knoll with a backcloth of fields, is charming, even to the law-abiding. A church was recorded in 1260, and indeed the list of rectors goes back that far, but the present building appears to be of the fifteenth century and even so was much restored - the chancel completely rebuilt - in Victorian times. The interior is intimate to the point of cosiness; the eighteenth century musicians' gallery, the corn dolly made from the last sheaf of the last wheat crop in Trentishoe, the photographs, the close-set pews.

Blackmoor Gate

Blackmoor Gate, to the motorist, is a reference point on the map, a place to stop for a meal or half-a-pint of beer. Until a few years ago it boasted a convenient garage and, before that, a hotel as well. (The hotel burnt down and the garage became redundant in changing times.) To the farmer it is the place where sheep are bought and sold, where trucks and trailers muddy the road on Mondays and where beer is drawn in pints. From the turn of the century till 1935 it was a railway station on the Lynton-Barnstaple line. Earlier still the stage-coach would stop there to pick up and set down passengers. It is, and probably always has been, a focal point, a staging post.

Though there may well have been, later, a toll gate in the vicinity of the modern cross roads, the original 'Blackmoor Gate' was probably a little to the south at the top of the rise on the South Molton road, marked on Ordnance Survey maps as 'Blackmoor Cross'. Westwards from here a road runs to Loxhore, a pleasant, winding country road with wide but variable grass verges - an old road. It passes through Wistlandpound and skirts a cluster of old farms - Huckham, Bess Hill, Brinscombe. It is the way Hugh Wichehalse took on his journey from Barnstaple and so carefully recorded - as far as West Land Pound the road was (by his standards) good but ahead lay the Black Moors. He and his cavalcade halted at the little inn in the hollow and then, refreshed, climbed uphill and plunged into the bleak moorland (or Black? It comes to the same thing; even now it is a surly place in winter.)

This was in 1628 but the road was old even then: Huckham at least is a Saxon name. Past Loxhore the road ran on to Shirwell, the seat of local Saxon administration, and on to Pilton, where King Alfred established a defensive 'burgh'. It is recorded that the burghs were interconnected; how else but by this road?

Gradually the farm fields would be extended to the limit imposed by the high moor; there would be a hedge or bank thrown round them, with a gate to accommodate the track - after all, sheep and cattle would be grazed on the moor in the summer. (And some cattle, or sheep, would stray, and be impounded just inside the reclaimed lands to the west of the moor-land, in the West Land Pound).

So Hugh Wichehalse, fortunately with a Lynton man as a guide, went through the gate on to the moor, crossing, presumably, on the way, the rudimentary track running inland from the coast. He, or his guide, then had a choice: one path led in a direct line to Parracombe, from where no easy route to Lynton existed; another led along the ridge, eventually joining the South Molton - Lynton road at Wood Barrow. He chose the former.

This route is again referred to in 1797, when it still seemed to be the regular way from Parracombe to Blackmoor Gate or beyond, before the toll road - later to become the A39 - was built. It can be traced very easily today, either from the map - a continuous hedge-line is shown from Blackmoor Cross to Rowley Cross, to be continued, without change of direction, as the road to the village - or on the ground - the hedge is seen to be accompanied by a wide and shallow hollow way, more distinct, as might be expected, in some parts than others.

But perhaps Hugh Wichehalse's rejected alternative is the more interesting. A hundred yards or so from the gate (a gate still hangs there) is a standing -stone, about three feet high, roughly triangular, set at an angle to the hedge - that is, to the old Parracombe way. The ground holds no sign of a track now but if the direction indicated by the stone is followed, the traveller finds himself on a very distinct ridge - such a distinct ridge, in fact, that no guiding track is needed - which is just as well as the land was found, after the relevant Enclosure Act, to be very good pasture and has been well ploughed, seeded and grazed ever since. The ridge, then, is easily followed and, being so followed, discloses in the next mile of two perhaps the richest display of archeological findings on Exmoor. Holwell Barrow, though the most imposing, is only one of numerous barrows along the way to Parracombe Two Gates: thereafter come Chapman's Barrows, the Long Stone, Longstone Barrow and yet two more before Wood Barrow.

Good written evidence that the route existed in mediaeval times; circumstantial evidence, surely, that it existed in the Bronze Age. Maybe it was even older, linked with the ancient ridgeways of the Stone Age.

Envoi

And so, in the end, it was not the herrings or the oysters, or the sheep, or the rye, but the majestic hills and the sea that saved Lynton.

In particular, perhaps, the coast. Take a boat out of Lynmouth harbour, past the Perch Pole and the Half-tide jetty, between the Weir posts (the eastern one marks the salmon weir), heading up channel with the flow of the tide. Give Blacklands Beach (once called Coal Pits, perhaps by charcoal burners) a wide berth and steer for Ninnywell where the oyster-catchers congregate, their handsome plumage and red beaks vivid against the rock. On to Sillery Sands, where the Vikings may (or may not) have landed and past Great Blackhead to Gunchamber, where the air trapped in the sea-level caves is expelled by the surf, on rough days, with explosive force. Skirting the Foreland ledges, where cormorants stand like sentinels, round the point with its twisted and tortured rock strata and (once, but no longer, under the watchful eyes of the lighthouse men) drift into Countisbury Pool. Here the view extends across Porlock Bay to Hurlstone Point, where the Devil challenged the Porlock Giant to a throwing match; closer at hand Rodney Cottage and, below it, Squire Halliday's lime kilns cling improbably to the cliff face.

Or go down on the ebb, as the old sailing boats would take care to do, across the bay to Ruddy Ball, whose name is amply justified when the sun sets behind it on a summer evening although it may stem from some old Celtic root. Under Ragged Jack, where Southey 'ascended with some toil, the highest point' and found peace there - though the more prosaic boatmen call the place 'Iron Railings' and use it as a mark for Half-Tide Rock. On to lichen-covered Yellow-stone, where Fulmar Petrels soar, and across Wringcliff Bay (taking a bearing on squire Bailey's Folly Tower on Duty Point to avoid Wringcliff Rock) to the sheer cliff from which the hapless but happily fictitious Jennifried flung herself, to Lee Bay with its lime kilns and summer bathers.

Under Crock Pits where, they say, the Dutchmen came to trade for clay until, one Sunday morning, it slid into the sea. Across Woody Bay, where confident men built a pier for steamers but reckoned without the northerly gales (though the older lime-kiln still stands) and round Wring-a-peak.

Round Wring-a-peak, disregarding the tide-race which flows like a river, to an enchanted world of cliffs and rocks and little caves, chosen place of guillemots and razorbills and kittiwakes and on, beneath the fort where Roman soldiers watched for invading tribesmen and beneath the coast-guard path where a later generation watched for smugglers and perhaps for Bonaparte's fleet, to Highveer. Braving Highveer's spray-swept rocks- and avoiding the lobster-pot lines - ease the boat into the little haven of Heddons Mouth, as countless seafarers have done before, in coracles, long-boats, luggers and who knows what other now forgotten craft.

About the Author

Dr. Mold came to live in Lynton in 1953 and continued to practice there as a local G.P. for thirty years. The practice extended from Kentisbury Ford to the top of Porlock Hill. In the early days, when transport was restricted, he took village surgeries and made extensive visiting rounds. In this way he came to know the district and its inhabitants intimately and he found time to talk with people whose local memories stretched back to the last century.